FORECAST

ESSENTIAL POETS SERIES 208

Canada Council for the Arts

Conseil des Arts du Canada

ONTARIO ARTS COUNCIL
CONSEIL DES ARTS DE L'ONTARIO

50 YEARS OF ONTARIO GOVERNMENT SUPPORT OF THE ARTS
50 ANS DE SOUTIEN DU GOUVERNEMENT DE L'ONTARIO AUX ARTS

Guernica Editions Inc. acknowledges the support of
the Canada Council for the Arts and the Ontario Arts Council.
The Ontario Arts Council is an agency of the Government of Ontario. We
acknowledge the financial support of the Government of Canada through
the Canada Book Fund (CBF) for our publishing activities.

For Susan —
Thanks for the inspiration!
Fond memories
of Ottawa... Clara Blackwood
♡ Oct. 1. 2016

FORECAST

Clara Blackwood

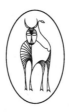

GUERNICA
TORONTO – BUFFALO – LANCASTER (U.K.)
2014

Michael Mirolla, editor
Elana Wolff, poetry editor
Guernica Editions Inc.
P.O. Box 76080, Abbey Market, Oakville, (ON), Canada L6M 3H5
2250 Military Road, Tonawanda, N.Y. 14150-6000 U.S.A.

Distributors:
University of Toronto Press Distribution,
5201 Dufferin Street, Toronto (ON), Canada M3H 5T8
Gazelle Book Services, White Cross Mills, High
Town, Lancaster LA1 4XS U.K.

Book design by Jamie Kerry of Belle Étoile Studios
www.belleetoilestudios.com

First edition.
Printed in Canada.

Legal Deposit – First Quarter

Library of Congress Catalog Card Number: 2013947103

Library and Archives Canada Cataloguing in Publication

Blackwood, Clara, 1976-, author
Forecast / Clara Blackwood.

(Essential poets series ; 208)
Poems.
Issued in print and electronic formats.
ISBN 978-1-55071-819-5 (pbk.).--ISBN 978-1-55071-820-1 (epub).--
ISBN 978-1-55071-821-8 (mobi)

I. Title. II. Series: Essential poets series ; 208

PS8553.L3248F67 2014   C811'.6   C2013-905520-7
C2013-905521-5

for Jane Estelle Trombley in memory
October 10, 1965 - January 25, 2013

Contents

THREE: A Possible Labyrinth

FOUR: Gift of Saturn

FIVE: Arcana

ONE

Stars in an Indigo Cosmos

The White Tower

I believe a strange force field surrounds
the high-rise I live in.
This would explain the insanity,
the jumpers, baby-danglers,
elevators opening between floors,
and my perilous love life.

It's not a force field that protects,
but revs things up, frenetic,
like too many nines in an address.

It explains the lady on the 14th floor,
cloaked in Edwardian,
who threw a butcher knife
down the length of the hallway.

I will witness the balconies bleeding blue,
the flying buttresses coming unhinged,
3 a.m. false alarms, urgent
knocks at my door asking for help.
I have my place in it.

Blind Date

A mouthful of roses, his laughter.
He has a good job, works out
at the gym more than I do.
His voice is deep
as his wine-coloured shirt.

Spontaneous risk-taker.
Loves skydiving,
has performed in adult films,

wears his Bluetooth to bed.

By evening's close
he tells me all about myself:
      I invite trouble,
      am a locked vault,

and I can't rectify any of it.

The Infatuation

In the storm of his hands
I saw a hint
of what was to come.
His words were satellites
I mistook for planets.

In the end I found
no topiaries,
no lakeshore.
Just an abandoned warehouse
in a back alley.

Change of Address

He lives above a haunted nightclub –
old site of an aboriginal curse.
After the bass subsides,
he hears the walls moan.

The rooms lie awake.
They house dealers and wendigos.

Sometimes the nightlife
continues upstairs;
a dominatrix flees at dawn,
her garter wilting on the doorknob.

Cinéma vérité

In the dream we are both
changing kitty litter,
scooping the refuse
into glossy white bags.

We are doing this simultaneously
in two identical apartments –
side by side
like a split-screen frame
in some French film.

I could never picture you
changing kitty litter,
yet here I meet you
in an oblique hallway
– true to dream –
plastic bag in hand.
Caught with the evidence.

Elegy for Eric

The ice cream trucks
have left the streets.
Looks like a long, cold winter.

— Eric Layman

Today the sun is a blazing white star —
hot enough to melt ice cream trucks.
Once the sun was golden,
not so harsh
as your sudden absence, which I can't block out.

Eric, let's meet for coffee at the Kensington Café,
talk poetry and politics,
though we won't agree.
I won't take offense —
I know no harm was meant.
It's just fraternal fire.

I'll bait you
about New Age (*rhymes with sewage*)
Islam (*never surrender to God*)
or moving to the suburbs (*let's bulldoze Don*
Mills and build cattle ranches!).

Will I ever again meet such
a radical libertarian
bohemian?

That an *atheist with a sense of wonder*
got along so well with this
mystically inclined sceptic
was a secular miracle.

You are the second archer
to descend – poet, close friend –
whose quicksilver mind
agitated complacency.

I *want you to be more ruthless,*
you urged –
by which you meant bold,
uncompromising.

I promise this.

Stellar Luminosity

Two sunflowers,
stars in an indigo cosmos.

One, a supergiant –
redder than Antares.

The other, a giant –
more orange than Arcturus.

They don't know about human activity,
or climate change here on earth;

how, unlike them, we use energy
as though it were inexhaustible

and we wouldn't find ourselves
outside the Main Sequence,

our own planet's future
foreshadowing the lifespan of the sun.

Three of Pentacles

Three talents,
three wishes,
three possibilities

encompassed by three disks.

I pass them between my hands,
knowing the outcome
is subject to change.
For I live in a house of threes.

The future unfolds
like the artisan's thread –
thread by threadbare
thread,

should I take this apprenticeship?

Pentacle-bright as Orion's belt
on a midwinter's night.

The Beginnings of Poetry

Because the tangerine floor,
        trap door, closed entrance.
Because of solitary rooms and a love of the hermetic.
Because of bullying.
Because it was never forced or encouraged.
Because of art school's salient critique.
Because loud and garrulous.
Because the throes of images.
        Book after book.
Because New Orleans, Dominican Republic, Horseshoe Bay.
Because early internet; insomnia.
Because the Free Times Café.
Because of momentary angels, accidental lightning.
Because of fallen matchsticks, cigarette ash and morning breath.
Orange-red afterglow.
Because of music's cruel abandonment at concert's end.
Because it is more elegant to wend desire through symbol.
Because language invents me:
        the pulse of throat, tickle of heart.
Because corrosion happens.
        Avalanche, blackouts, words in Braille.
Because Pluto was demoted from planet.
Because the cosmic microwave background.
Because photons dance off my palms,
        past the fry pan.
Because eating a double chocolate scoop of the universe, whole.
Because I coalesce, then contradict.
        Too small to fit inside seasons.
Because the harbour turned me away.
Because eyes dipped in silver watched over the bedside table.
Because loss.

Because hearing.
Because essential to abrade surface.
Because tenacious near death, hovering above my body.
Because of surgery.
      Night-blue buses.
Because the twist.

Forecast

The weather ahead is unpredictable.

Shellfish could fall from the skies,
summer and winter
congeal.

You may find love,
or spite. Always ambivalence.

There are wind patterns you don't understand,
pink hailstones and midnight at noon.
Total solar eclipse,
birds migrating in reverse.

You believe there is a way
to distil chaos; that you could recover
a torch to illuminate the darkness,
pinpoint a light source
brighter than Andromeda.

If you just knew how to begin.

Two

Shifting into Cerulean

CLARA BLACKWOOD

Local Pantheon

Today the ravine teems with life:
crows chase hawks, foxes hunt hares,
the dam overflows and something
shimmers between the trees.

Each blade of grass
aware of itself.

The animal spirits from long ago
made an agreement.
The human imprint
has yet to unseat it.

Lies and Secrets

*These spirits are my awful companions;
I can't tell anyone when they move in me.*

— Gwendolyn MacEwen

I can't tell anyone
about the secrets and lies,
the ways of becoming, of influence
that transform this mere vessel
into a larger sum.
It's a kind of blind vision,
divine dissonance
involving conjurations,
auguries and enchantments –
making the world from sand.

I can't tell anyone
that I am not entirely alone,
even if I'd like to be.
It's a kind of existential pantheism,
a cacophony of deities at centre
clamouring for attention
intrepid as birds of prey,
that stalk my evenings
like owl eyes staring out of green –
or the great panther rarely seen.

Asphodel

I sensed a looming,
swore I saw black waters
flowing beneath my feet
when a dark figure
returned to my dreams,
recurred in my Tarot readings –
his uninvited silhouette at the door.

Nature is your Goddess.
She listens as you crack open the earth,
emerge from cheerless caverns.
And I could be that abducted maiden,
from long ago, taken down,
down.

I am accustomed to phantom spaces,
wrong turns.
November's funereal drift.
The westerly wind calling me to
a forgetting.

I would gladly make the descent,
if only
you were willing
to share the power.

Your beckoning hand
candles the air.
Between two pillars far underground,
amongst the asphodels.

Five of Wands

In the future position this card
shows a great green dragon
with prickly wings
guarding an expectant treasure.
In the foreground, Jason and Medea,
brandishing wands,
rush toward him.

I cannot tell if the beast at hand
represents you or me,
or whether we are the couple.

We have become so similar
in our ire –
neither one willing
to lower our weapons.

And I begin to wonder if compromise
is a betrayal –
or can the Golden Fleece
be gained by negotiation?

Not knowing, I pray
for the dragon's lambent flight,
the glimpse of an orange opening.
Not the flames.
Not five crimson tears.

Compass

The whirlpool brought me here
on one of Hokusai's waves.
I know this watery realm
from elsewhere.

Within the turquoise deep
something stirs.
The Hydra could live here,
though I've heard her stature
is much diminished.

I don't know where I am –
Japan?
I could swear this is the blue
Pacific,
but my body is a faulty compass.

I'm recalling
submerged cities, capsized boats.
A single steeple
all that remains of a
once pre-eminent town.

The lighthouse ahead
(one my grandmother knew)
suddenly
vanishes from view.

Daphne Speaks

Dream of me before,
dream of me after,
waves crashing on some remembered beach –
such was my freedom.

Your marble face
emerges from cloudtop,
gazes earthward
at my gnarled form.

You would have chased me
into mist and sky –
anywhere to trap
this huntress.

The river god has served me well.
Few recognize my laurel likeness.
To those who understand,
I speak in sand dollars.

Tower Interior

1.

It is surprising you so quickly
and willingly found the tower –
walked right up to its double doors,
opened them, peered within.

It is one thing to locate the tower,
nestled in a nameless valley,
hidden by a mountain range.
Another to see its interior.

It houses many actors,
each on his and her own floor.
The flighty, the infatuated,
the furious, the terrified.
They scream at different hours.

2.

An elaborate banquet hall stands
at the circular centre. Sixteen gold plates
anticipating a feast. Burgundy walls
adorn the foyer, familiar
as the taste of eggplant.

The second-most prized room,
entered only from behind a bookcase,
is a sanctum where the muse is summoned.

A troupe of dancers entertained here,
before withdrawing into the foothills.

Some say they had bad luck,
others great fortune.

The valley is protective of its stories.

The Woman and the Anchor

Before her is a great expanse of unknown.
Nothing but vagueness.

She stands on a rocky cliff,
wind-lashed,
wanting to leave this place,
stuck.

She is trying to lift
a giant anchor,
twice her size.
It's futile.

She imagines
strong arms
coming to her aid.

Years pass like clouds.

One day without effort
she tosses the anchor
into the sea.

In the far distance
a ship
unfurls its sails.

Two Kinds of Blue

Today the blueness burns
inbetween new greens and space's
soundless blackness.

— Margaret Avison

My life is changing.
No more the cyan it once was.
Shifting into cerulean.

A band of white
divides the two phases:
what I can't know and the inevitable.

A deeper blue burns
in the beholding eye.
Soft blacks compel the perimeter.

Here I must make space
for the new —
sky emptying into stream.

What binds me together are ciphers,
scratched in the fabric
of now.

Compatriot

Those planes crashing into the towers
weren't real, he tells me.
They were holograms.

I've been told many strange things
over the years;
this is one of the strangest.

He's giving a speech
at the conference on 9/11 Truth,
I should go.
I've not been *intellectually responsible*.

And the conversation soon shifts –
to one I have no say in.
Eisenhower. Aliens. The Bilderbergers.
Illuminati. Weather Control Agents.

Global Warming is a hoax, don't you know?

He throws me a cavalcade of creatures.
Each wears a false face,
hiding a fake flag.
The podium of power keeps shifting,
covering up their vile plots of world domination.

Who is the main bogeyman?
        The reptiles, apparently.

He flashes a chlorine-titled paperback
long enough for me to read –

Children of the Matrix: How an Interdimensional
Race has Controlled the World for Thousands
of Years – and Still Does.

The cover bears a reptilian eye
merged with a human iris.
Its unblinking gaze
follows me home.

Passenger

I'm given a general description:
Look for a champagne Mercury
at the Kiss 'n' Ride,
two girls in the back.

I spot my vehicle,
flinch for a second.
Maybe I shouldn't get in the car
with strangers,
though the driver is a woman.

She's friendly, warm,
violet eyeshadow extended to the brow.
Long, pink claws pinching the steering wheel.

Once we hit the road,
she floors the pedal
and we speed to the glass tower.

Destination – a workshop,
Finding Your True Career.
On arrival
it's a lecture –
how to get rich quick with the law of attraction.

I excuse myself,
nearly trip over a crystal fountain
on the way to the bathroom;
notice the wall of copied U.S. bills above the toilet.
Anthony Robbins smiling
from the magazine rack.

Back at the gathering
the speaker scolds me
for using non-committal language:
if instead of
when I'm rich and happy.

The crowd applauds her.

THREE:

A Possible Labyrinth

Fire Scrying

She says she has fire in her
and you believe it;
wouldn't want to cross her.

Her rage is devastating,
an inescapable desert sun –
Medea in her blazing chariot,
scorching anything in her path.

She can make all kinds of fire –
green, white, blue –
send fire burning across water,
flash it away.

You've gazed into her bowl
of flames, seen faces,
whirling wheels and hands,
caught glimpses of your life ahead.

And you keep wondering
what her part will be –
how many of those flaming fingers
are hers.

Dreaming of Dragons

I've been dreaming of dragons lately –
cosmic, seafaring, earthy,
   everything dragons,
and I don't know what to think.

My best friend tells me
they're mostly incorporeal –
ambassadors for good or ill,
emblems of sexuality.

Last night, a dragon slumbering
in a diamond mine
was jarred awake by jackhammers
Deeply offended, he fled to
the nearest village, to stir up support
for a ban on excavations.

In another dream, a dragon
emerged from a lake,
and tore through the landscape,
dragging hydro lines and houses
like tin cans
behind a *Just Married* car.

I've been dreaming of dragons
and I don't know what to think.
Each morning under my pillow,
I find pearly scales,
        incandescent eggs,
                indigo teeth.

Somewhere a dragon is dreaming me.

Eight of Swords

A circle of swords radiates
like a maze around me.
An abandoned castle, high on a cliff,
looms at my back.

I had to leave that fortress
though its confines
provided security,
a view of a marshland
that would one day sink me completely.

And I hear your voice,
mirroring steel –
Go save your own damn self!

I was waiting my turn to be rescued.

Witness the recovery of stones,
the rounding of corners.

The pathway forward,
a possible labyrinth.

Edge of Edinburgh

I. *Newhailes*

Grey against blue it rises,
a cherry tree on either side,
triumph of 18th century symmetry.
A mansion balanced and illustrious
like the bewigged men who visited here
during the Scottish Enlightenment.
They would have scoffed
at my superstitious ways.

I'm reading *The Ghost*
That Haunted Itself,
spooking myself before bed,
pulling the tartan blanket
tight over my head.

Two ghost tours
and I haven't seen a spectre.
Not sure I want to,
if it's one that leaves scratch marks.

Catholic friends gift me
a flask of holy water.

II. *Old Town*

At every cobblestone turn,
the site of some grisly historic fact.

Here – the public scaffold.
There – the tavern hangout
for body snatchers.

Cafés, pubs and closes
named after morbid figures.

Villains strangely canonized.

III. *Greyfriars Kirkyard*

A Thin Place.
Thinner at 3 a.m.
or equinox, at Hallows,
when King Death rules supreme,
peers out from tombstones, grinning.
Tears the veil of this world and that.

I'm gathered with strangers –
the psychically-inclined or curious.
Our overzealous guide scares us
with tales of possession,
insanity and sudden collapses.

We wait by the graveyard's
black gates.

Was that a cold spot I just felt,
or Scotland's changeable weather?

By twilight's end,
not one of us is going in.

IV. *The Witches' Well*

I wandered the Castle Esplanade,
searching the four directions,
treading the cobblestone path,
without any luck beneath my feet.

A guide pointed the way:
northwest,
toward the base of the Hill.
Not a well, but a fountain.

Elevated on a stone wall
it dwells modestly, not a place
for wishes.
Commemoration.

Through the centuries, hundreds
were burned alive here.
Were they truly wise,
or hated outcasts?

From the iron panel,
entangled in foxglove and snake, two faces
emerge – the benevolent maiden,
the maligned crone.

The left side reads, *The Evil Eye*,
the right, *Hands of Healing*.
Violets bloom from tended soil
near the fountain's basin.

V. *Lady Glamis, 1537*

Burnt at the stake
with husband and son as witnesses,
the lady cannot rest.

Through a rare ability reserved
for saints – to *bilocate* –
she haunts both Edinburgh
and Glamis Castles.

In life, she faced tragedy.
In death, she achieves
a ghostly beatitude.

VI. *Last Night in Edinburgh*

I am not sure why you called me spooky.
Far more inexplicable things
were happening that evening –
the candle extinguishing itself,
the scent of anise infusing the room
from nowhere.

Outside, it was well past equinox,
the fog had dispersed, and all was quiet
along the Royal Mile.

You pointed out a red bird
on the rooftop, saying this was a good omen –
that he was some kind of guardian
and all would be well.
I was not assured.

To the hotel at Castlehill
I returned, sensing trouble,
and asked for protection.

Like a Scottish *caim*
I pictured myself surrounded by light,
impermeable to devious intent,
reminding myself
I am safe.

North Berwick

This seaside town fell
under the suspicion of James VI.
Rumours flourished of magic
on the beach, storms conjured
to drown the King as he sailed
home from Denmark.
Were the accused dancing
on the Auld Kirk Green?
Perhaps.

Standing on the strand, the wind
pulls my hair, and I taste iodine.
Bladderwrack covers the shore
like a green shawl.
Weather-beaten Tantallon
lies three miles east,
concealed by craggy coast.
The sea, a preternatural blue.

Near the gentle walkway, traffic
slows like a merry-go-round.
I get lost in the stone-fronted streets,
blackened with time.
The antique shop displays
a mirror inside a mirror,
pillbox hats with veils.
Where are the witches of North Berwick
today?

Malcolm

It's two parts nostalgia,
one part gothic commitment
that we're dressed like the Addams Family –
burgundy lips on the hunt for a Goth club
in Edinburgh.

The evening's agenda:
some organ music – aperitif
before the shadowy dance –
ideally in an underground chamber
or dungeon.

We take our seats in the nave of the church
when a stranger approaches.

He looks like Keats – long curls
falling on a poet's blouse, eyes
worn from introspection.
Burnt sienna blazer matching
the wood of the pipe organ.

His favourite poets?
Shelley, Byron, Baudelaire.
Barely anyone from the 20th century.
Poetry ends with Eliot.

He works for Historic Scotland.
I picture him among castle ruins,
a sunset glow on sandstone towers
as he bids farewell to the last tourists
and contemplates his modern ennui.

At twenty-six, he tells us, he's too old
for the Goth bars but he'll recommend
a few places if that's what we're into.

He compliments our black dresses,
asks how long we're in town,
and when I say till tomorrow,
he looks confused, says nothing more.

Before the concert begins, he drifts
to the front of the stage, then disappears
into the plush red velvet.

Glasgow →Iceland → Toronto

My fate rests in the plumes
of an ash cloud:
a giant piece of black cauliflower
dominating the world news
and atmospheric conditions over Europe.

At Glasgow Airport I read *Cancelled*
all down the terminal screen,
one long red blur until
the last flight: Toronto.
The only one scheduled to leave.

Ten minutes before departure
Queen's "A Kind of Magic"
plays through the Thomas Cook airways
and I think, Yes, this *is* a kind of magic
that I'm here on this cushy, blue seat,
not exiled to a sleeping mat,
calling loved ones in a panic.

The song ends and the captain
tells us a change of route is necessary –
we'll head directly for Iceland,
fly around the ash cloud.
Keep your fingers crossed for clear skies.

Next, "Under Pressure" begins
to pulse and I wonder, Is this deliberate
on the part of the crew?
Some kind of prophecy?

I glance at the woman beside me
reading the paper:
Ash cloud chaos hits UK.
She doesn't look nervous
or alarmed that disorder's taken reign.

And just when
"Another One Bites the Dust" begins,
I've had enough of this musical fortunetelling.

Irish Witches

An Irish witch requires no effort crossing over. She's already halfway to Summerland – consorting with angels, demons, Celtic gods, and her deceased great aunt on the O'Leary side.

An Irish witch chooses Yeats as her familiar, conjures him to appear, and then changes his human form.

Irish witches aren't like the English – cooped up in damp estates. Or those American witches who bring cell phones to ritual.

An Irish witch wears the land as her second skin, visits the sea daily. And when she returns home, the tides miss her.

Irish witches rarely use dating sites, and if they do, only niche ones. Sure they'll have you over to the cottage for tea and soda bread – if they like the lilt in your voice. But you must ask yourself: Is the cat huddled by the fireplace really a cat?

Four:

Gift of Saturn

Prescient

Once again you appear
at the gates of horn and ivory,
white powder below the nose
telling me you've been up to no good.

Before us, a wide, glass table
in a barren room,
a calamity of walls.

Though we haven't spoken in years,
I hear the rumours: new schemes –
and charges laid, travel
across a transient sky.

Footsteps falling from the roof.

At the Corner of Queen and Claremont

Word of its existence reached me
through high school corridors:
tales of bloodletting, vampires,
paranormal feats.

There was a place, a nightclub,
beyond my Anne Rice dreams.

I donned a black dress and eyeliner.
White pancake makeup.
Made my way from the 'burbs
to gothic downtown.

Werewolves and sirens congregated
inside the cavernous walls.
Walls as wide as lovers' eyes:
the voice of Andrew Eldritch,
definite as jet.

The undead wearing chain mail,
PVC and corsets.
Dry ice pooling on the legions of feet.
Flash of a silver pentacle
below a freshly bitten neck.

You could lose yourself
in the pulsating lights –
fall into trance and not return.
Or wake up on the other side of desire.

Anonymous

A headless woman waits outside my door.
Some art student or insomniac
must have left her there, fully
aware of my papier-mâché phobia.

Bright coloured and life-sized
she's a human piñata
with one arm broken off.

And she was made deliberately headless –
the neck-stump painted a crude coral.

Black lines descend from her shoulders –
prison bars
with no one behind them.

Three dusty flowers dangle
from her wrist attached with twine
like executioner's rope.

I take her to the curbside where she
scares the starlings away.
With the city's new bylaws, garbage collectors
won't touch her.

In the Sun Garden

You would enter my life after
a period of turmoil –
bad fortune, loss,
romantic despair.
I felt the night-terrors,
even at summer's peak.

Your presence dispels fear,
casts a halo of yellow.
Nothing that's revealed
changes your loyalty.
We stand tall as sunflowers
in daylight's grace.

Water-bearer

You bring me orchids, ambrosia:
two bottles – one white, one red.
In your liquid eyes I see
black onyx, horses pacing at night.
And I have all these questions:
What do you know
about the Bermuda triangle?
Do you believe in destiny, fixed stars,
divine intervention?
                              But I let them go.

I've shed another skin. Abandoned old ways.
Yes, we've lived the traumas,
betrayals and vendettas –
but we won't let them claim us.
I release vindictiveness,
let it fall serpentine from my fingers
for the earth to eat.

Long Island Medium

She could be mistaken for any random
loud-mouthed extrovert
with an excessive love of hairspray –
her bleached blonde coif
stiff as dry bread.
And her nails, talons,
precede her screeching voice.

Not what you might expect
for someone who speaks to the dead.

Incredulity sets in
till it becomes apparent
she's legit.

Booked a year in advance
for consultations, she makes
the nascent psychic
in me jealous.

But she says Don't worry,
when the snow flies
your readings will thrive.

Her husband is the perfect foil.
Earthy and muscular, he tends
the domestic domain, looks after
cooking, chores, gardening,
whatever needs to be done at the house.
Is without want of the uncanny.

I sit in her famous dining room,
the place where furniture has moved
on its own,
breathe deeply the scent of lilies.
As she pours full moon water
into a stone bowl,
ancestors crowd the hallway.

A Victorian Life

My life began drearily –
daughter of a minor clerk
and a woman who died in childbirth.
At twenty, courted by a melancholic
who threatened suicide if we didn't marry.
Tired of dragging my petticoats through sludge,
I acquiesced.
We were happy for a while –
until he began to frequent brothels.
Soon after his precious angel
became a lunatic whore.

Cast adrift, I discovered
the bohemian circle – artist faces
gloomy as the maroon of parlour walls.
I dabbled in theosophy, spiritualism,
joined a secret society –
an offshoot of the Golden Dawn.
Had an affair with a magus.
We were mad for each other, twin souls,
and shortly thereafter
my husband died.
I was accused of murder.

Plagued by peculiar nightmares,
I fled to Canada and crossed it by rail –
registering under a pseudonym
at the Empress Hotel.

Visitors come and go.
Daily I read tea leaves for signs

of the approaching century:
>> a raven perched on a cross,
>> a sword piercing a cloud.

Dream Notes on the King of the Faeries

He has high cheekbones,
a sharp jawline and arched eyebrows.
Dark brown hair and hazel eyes.
There's an air of caprice,
also inquisitiveness.
His hand reaches into the foxglove, again.

*

The Page of Cups, with pointed features,
drops falling from the tips of long fingers
as he offers the cup of invitation and proposals.
The triumphant return of the Elf King
in a hyper-modern world.
He arrives alone, to dance
under multi-coloured lights,
moves in sync, yet ahead of the music.
Dances in my dream in Faerie,
cascades of gas flame blue,
iridescence behind him.

*

I stumble upon a troop of them,
playing instruments, singing.
The one with the hummingbird wings,
spinning in mid-air,
displaying great joy,
first catches my attention.
He, tallest of all,
appears to be leading this Pixie fair.

*

Suddenly, they all make strange,
realize they're being watched.
Halt the merrymaking,
become sullen,
sombre.

*

Elsewhere, Vulcan at his forge.
Experiments go awry,
cause fires and explosions downtown.
He's been on trial for public mischief,
is hated by many,
but he's most at home
undone by greater rapture.
His skinny ribcage fills with air,
and his whole body shakes ecstatically,
in rhythmical motions
following the lead
of his Priestess partner.

Ten of Cups

For so long it hid from you –
the sapphire-encrusted
grail you hoped for,
wanting to drink from a cup
just out of reach.

Marriage, it was predicted,
would come late. No impetuous wish
could speed the process.
This was the gift of Saturn.

And here you are,
family at forty.
adopted son,
daughter of your own.

Venture capitalist, world traveller:
the man you married
grew up two blocks from you –
in the country of your birth.

Now the Pacific in your backyard,
tennis court by the water's edge,
a line of clothing in your name.
Vineyard, brimming.

As you sit in your Marine Drive home,
glass of Merlot in hand,
you realize you've achieved the fantasy.
Palm trees sway in breaking cascade.

A mile away from the fault line.

Confessions of a Self-help Addict

No more psychotherapy,
I've taken matters into my own hands.
Well-being is destiny.
The world does not exist beyond
my inner self. I am
a self-help addict.

Don't tell my family
I've spent my inheritance
on motivational retreats.
I chant: You are what you think!
You can have it all! Quitters never win!
And believe me, I won't quit.

I own all 21,647 self-help books
on Amazon.com.
Chapter by chapter I dive
into repressed memory, lose pounds
just thinking about my childhood.

I discover my Personal Power
while operating heavy equipment.
I listen to Dr. Phil
on my iPod in the shower.

I'm evolving.
Have decided to love all my exes
unconditionally –
but only after they live up to their full potential.

I'm guilt-free, actualized,
yelling:
Don't sweat the small stuff!
to anyone having a meltdown.

I'm moving forward. Leaving behind
the co-dependents, enablers,
anger-repressors, and anyone
who speaks from negativity –
they're confined to my closet.

No one comes between
me and my self-esteem.

FIVE:

Arcana

O. The Fool

I am the breath of first sun –
wide open.
Green is my song.

Find me along the cliffside,
anywhere near the moment
of dissolve.

I ascend mountains
holding a white rose,
the clouds my captors.

I need not male or female.
I am both
and neither.

My sole companion,
a wildcat, warns me
when I miss the butterfly.

I. The Magician

He stands, brilliant in starlight,
a rainbow ending in the palm
of his hand.

The art of fascination
is his, and the coveted grace.

Red birds dive into his white robe.

Infinity before him.

And you wish he wouldn't so often
confuse ego with self.

The High Priestess
is his counterpart and ally.
But he could forfeit
even her.

II. The High Priestess

Think her oblique,
like Temple pillars
subtly slanted upwards
or the north door concealed
in an old church.

She is the guardian of transparency –
keeper of worlds
we can't talk about.

Over her a fine mesh
falls. From certain angles
the diadem shines silver-bright.

She has eaten from the pomegranate,
danced with the Daughters of Night.

And she is the one
who appears when your feet
stomp out the bonfire.

III. The Empress

Without her I would be
a particle of dust
settling on a concrete slab.

Instead, the handle turns.
Mauve doors open upon mauve doors
opening into gardens.

First, a coronation of swans.
Then, her forehead radiant from
the garland of twelve stars.

She is present, always,
in the powdered sky.
Pregnant with thrones,

denominations.
I move within her too,
know I am also wing.

Teach me, torch-bearer,
grant me passage.

IV. The Emperor

Once, you frightened me.
With one fell stare, you'd condemn,
or at best, dismiss.

Seated on your carved throne
you are as immovable
as granite.

I've felt the rage of your inquisition,
believed you the source
of that sterile tyrant – rationality.

One hand grips a burnished sceptre,
the other inflames a globe.
You'd make the world chrome.

Father, under your sway
I see a dominated, pillaged earth,
materialism its god.

When you chopped down the tree
of Ashtoreth, you stirred
the wrath of elements.

The old empire is perishing.
Temper your strength with understanding,
or be exiled.

V. The Hierophant

He inhabits a secret
beyond the black and white
chequered floor,
between two grey pillars.

Around him are the masks
of misrule, the faces
of benediction.

Lion, bull, man, eagle –
he knows them all.

Friend of the blue Venus,
this hushed speaker
halts the unprepared
with one hand held in symbol.

To the seeker
he grants two golden keys,
but will not tell
what they unlock.

VI. The Lovers

Two women stand on either side –
one close to your age,
the other a matron.

Legend has it you must steal
from one to gain the favour
of the other.

I waited in the plume of night,
counting blessings in a glass house,
far from the valley of reckoning.

The sun came up,
the angel appeared,
you made your choice
(though I do share the same
birthday as your mother).

You will stay with me
in this transparent city
and not return to the isle
of your ancestors.

VII. The Chariot

At the helm stands
a sturdy charioteer,
or rather, the illusion of one.

Inflexible golden armour
with moons for shoulders –
like you and your carefully
crafted persona.

When you see your image
in the reflective shield,
the chariot gathers speed.

I fear to ask just where
the red-spoked wheels are taking you.

Certainly beyond this country's
soft borders, to where all
is vehemence
and error.

VIII. Strength

The south wind heralds your arrival,
tells of assured success.

You will dance under a marigold sun,
celebrate the lion.

Yours is the gaze of unwavering eyes
and the voice of ancient places –
pyramids and earthly fire.

Soon they will wreathe you with flowers,
in the yellow and green of your making,

for you broke the Corinthian column
to which you were bound.

It is August and your hands
are no longer covered in dust.

IX. The Hermit

The mountaintop is not lonely,
it's a resting place, far
from distractions.

In the city, I kept my light
within, moved in subtle circles.
My knowledge not a commodity.

Even with my lamp veiled,
strangers sought me out.

Occasionally I'd reveal *something*,
open my mantle in dark times,
hold up a looking glass –
but people almost never
see themselves.

There are three kinds
of light – creative,
reflective, and from above –

mirrored by three worlds.
One is harder to attain,
and tastes of licorice.

X. Fortune

Goddess Fortuna is a fickle mistress, don't pin your hopes on her.
She stands hoodwinked atop a giant wheel, sensing the rotary
motion under her toes, cool as porcelain. The laws which apply
to her do not apply to us. As has oft been said: *Change is the only
thing we can be certain of.*

In the end it's just me and a deck of tarot cards – laying the
spread, interpreting the symbols (although 98% of the time,
people ask about love or money, so there's some certainty
in that). I'm surprised I don't hear: *What is it I really want to do?
What are my hidden talents?*

And I think of the parable about the man who was given one
talent and buried it in the earth. Then spent his eternity in
a place with no light, only the weeping and gnashing of teeth.

Fortune's wheel
continues to spin,

whether we waste our talents
                    or not,
fulfil our will
                    or not,
take off the blindfold
                    or not.

So what is it you *really* want?

XI. Justice

When your days are ended,
will your heart be feather-light,
or like a sunken ship, its bulk
fed to the Devouress?

Yes, it comes down to a blade
held to the skull, the line
drawn in vermilion.

Do not fear.

You wield the sword,
maintain equilibrium.

Fortified, you travel the skies
like a sun god guided
by his twin sister.

Ibises appear at the equinox,
the moment of crisis
just before you change
from light to shade.

XII. The Hanged Man

Was it the Pythoness
who placed you there?
Was it the shadow?

For nine nights upside-down
you hung from a windy tree
letting the masks fall,
left foot dangling
from the world thread.

And you told yourself:
No *more disguises,*
I *can't bear this standstill anymore.*

Your memories, phthalo blue,
were of sea levels rising.
The waterfront, putrid.
Smell of decaying flesh.

Over time your face became
a nimbus, intensifying,
no longer the lamp
under the bushel
for none to know,

and gradually the living branch
let go –
leaving you
the sole captor
of your brilliant, innocuous mind.

XIII. Death

He trailed across the vault of night,
wrestled demons in high places.

He exploded in a starburst.
Stole the pearl within.

From the far reaches of space
to blue-green depth, the scythe
of his shadow passes.

But not to have loved him.

Not to have known him.

To see the city horizon
from the balcony's edge
hacked away like sugarcane.

All with her. Already with her.
The dark-haired woman awaiting him.

This is the final pain he causes me,
and the last time I linger.

XIV. Temperance

I've touched serenity –
the alchemical fusion
of fire and water,
peace between extremes.
But not today.

The guide who watches us
through sleep and meditation
has fled, leaving
one umber feather
outside the bedroom door.

You've said
you like fiery women
and I've said
you must accept
what that entails.

I am not the archangel
who mixes liquid to perfection.
More like Iris, I offer
a spectrum of experience.

The paranormal crown
my love ignites
will weigh on everything you do.

XV. The Devil

In the din and cold
I wished for a match.
The north wind offered up
a trail of smoke.

*Do you take this man
in his totality?*
I do.

Love soon opened a door.
We were shown
splendour, wilderness, heights.

When I met your shadow,
I shook hands with it.
Accepted fate.

And there, in your indigo heart,
sat the devil.

How could I know
you would flee what frees you,
to dig yourself another deep pit?

Answer me, my enemy-ally,
unlover, lord
of the underhand.

XVI. The Tower

I awoke to find
strange rubble at my feet,
and beneath a shattered sky
a landscape I no longer recognize.

How stealthily you come to decision.
Your disappearance,
cloaked in secrecy.

   Here
is an unfriendly place.
Arid, acrid. Neither fish
nor fowl can exist.

What is left – only
ashen trinkets.

Alecto, Magaera, Tisiphone –
sisters of retribution,
Daughters of Night,
I call upon you now.

Sandstorms obscure
my vision while stones
form empty reliquaries at my knees.

What is this language you speak?
I know it not –
your words strain upwards like false towers.

What is this creed you follow?
I don't believe in it –
your will against mine.

I stand before you again,
lightning-struck
and red with betrayal.

XVII. The Star

I was once shown the sphere
of the holy guardian angel,
a world within a world,
windless, without strife.

The nightingale lives there,
singing her rapturous song.

In my melancholy,
it has been revealed again,
by her who descends
when desire and prayer
call out unremittingly.

She walks the earth in many forms,
pouring an elixir
from twin pitchers.

I drink deep
like a tree in the desert
under watchful stars.

XVIII. The Moon

Journeyers past have been caught up
in illusion, sleepwalking
towards their graves,
drawn off like drops of moisture
to the glorious moon.

I see those drops before me now,
yod-shaped, leading down
the path to submersion.

They are the parts of my
neglected selves
longing for union.

Separation ails them; they
lose touch, become voices
walled off in watchtowers
that can't hear each other scream.

I must make a commitment.
Timing is slim.
Failure of nerve is
a flood pouring in.

XIX. The Sun

Lucky is he who stands unconstrained
on the grassy hill,
surrounded by the zodiac,
never losing his centre.

Terrible to be a house
divided, talents buried,
nothing but shadows
obscuring the self.

A temple at full capacity
makes for the best worship.
The gods in us are strengthened
by our belief.

Tell the messenger
fragrant with bay leaf
that I have vanquished division
and taken up residence at Heliopolis.

XX. Judgement

Hanging from the sky
a scarlet cross heralds
the final trumpet.

Beyond the open graves there is
both celebration
and a summons.

Magician and Priestess make amends.

The archangel draws near.

Gabriel's light
shines brightest on
the numinous child.

It is his time, our time.

XXI. The World

Civilizations come and go,
prophets, seers, invaders and end times,
but you will find me – a constant –
the figure inside the mandorla.

It was I who brought forth
sun, moon, planets, stars,
high tides, crystal caves,
turtles and mountain lions,
pandas and pythons,
circadian rhythms of tamarind trees.

And now there is war
on every corner.

When this world is destroyed,
I shall make another.
Create it from lapis lazuli.

Heed my words –
be true to your gifts,
follow them to my high castle
where I grant you
the necklace of rebirth.

Epilogue: The Aeon

Behind a covering of smog, a trumpet blares, joyous
and terrifying. We cannot see the trumpet, but we feel it
keen as dragon's teeth. There is gold, black and silver
in our blood. Scarlet in the belly. Many of us still carry
on as usual – precarious exploits in a void. It is time to
answer that call, raise our arms, forming the letter *Shin*.

In this fire age, the signs are all around. The hottest year
on record. The Middle East ablaze. Extremes of all kinds.
More severe storms and floods. Fires in need of cooling;
fires in need of fanning. Hot or cold, make a choice – now.
What you think, happens. Latent abilities become
manifest. Finally, the hidden talent unearthed. Falcon
hears the falconer. The falcon-headed god returns.

NOTES

The epigraph for "Elegy for Eric" is from Eric Layman's poem "The Ice Cream Trucks," published in the chapbook *The Brightest Fire* (Aeolus House). The poem is at ericlayman. blogspot.ca/p/poems-g-j.html. The phrase *"atheist with a sense of wonder"* is how Eric described his religious views.

"Main Sequence" in "Stellar Luminosity" is an astronomical term referring to a prominent and continuous band of stars that appear on an H-R diagram. Main-sequence stars release energy by fusing hydrogen into helium in their cores.

The inspiration for "Five of Wands" was gleaned from a tarot reading which included that very card from The Mythic Tarot deck.

The paperback mentioned in "Compatriot" is *Children of the Matrix: How an Interdimensional Race Has Controlled the World for Thousands of Years – and Still Does* by David Icke.

Newhailes from "Edge of Edinburgh" is the name of a neo-Palladian villa in Musselburgh, Scotland, just outside of Edinburgh.

The Ghost That Haunted Itself by Jan-Andrew Henderson is the story of the "Mackenzie Poltergeist" tied to Greyfriars Kirkyard.

Greyfriars Kirkyard is a cemetery established in 1561 in the Old Town of Edinburgh and reputed to be haunted.

The Witches' Well was erected in 1894 on the same spot where 300 women were burned alive as witches between 1479 and 1722.

In *Last Night in Edinburgh* the word "caim" (pronounced "kyem") is Scottish-Gaelic for "sanctuary." It is an invisible circle of protection, drawn around the body with the hand.

The line "*Walls as wide as lovers' eyes*" in "At the Corner of Queen and Claremont" is from the song "Temple of Love" by The Sisters of Mercy.

"Faerie" in "Dream Notes on the King of the Faeries" is the name for the world of Faerie.

In "Epilogue: The Aeon," *Shin* is the 21st letter of the Hebrew alphabet; it sounds like "sh" or "s."

Acknowledgements

Some of the poems in this collection first appeared in the following publications and websites: *Rampike*, *Quills*, *Dreamcatcher* (UK), *Carousel*, *Misunderstandings Magazine*, *Hart House Review*, chizinepub.com and cyclamensandswords.com. Many thanks to the editors.

"Fire Scrying" was published in the chapbook *Visitations* (Believe Your Own Press, 2004).

"Irish Witches" is for Sandra Kasturi, whose poem "Estonian Witches" was the source of inspiration.

"Compass," "Daphne Speaks," "Tower Interior," and "Two Kinds of Blue" were written in response to the respective works of artists Barbara Feith, Mary Lou Payzant, Gail Read, and Beryl Goering. Thank you to all the studio artists at the Women's Art Association of Canada for a fruitful collaboration.

Part Five of this book was originally published in the chapbook *Arcana* (Aeolus House, 2012).

Thank you to my publisher, Guernica Editions, for nurturing and having faith in this second longer collection. Heartfelt thanks to Elana Wolff, dream editor, for her tireless and thoughtful work on this manuscript. I am very fortunate to have worked with her a second time.

Thanks to my colleagues and friends in my two poetry workshops for their feedback and support. From the Muse

Co-operative: Sue Bowness, David Clink, Kate Marshall Flaherty, Yaqoob Ghaznavi, Joel Giroux, Valérie C. Kaelin, Sandra Kasturi and Francine Lewis. From The Long Dash group: Merle Nudelman, John Oughton, Mary Lou Soutar-Hynes, Sheila Stewart and Elana Wolff.

I am especially grateful to Rob Colman, Dane Swan and Myna Wallin for their generous feedback and vision that helped shape this collection; and to Phlip Arima, Sonia Di Placido, Katerina Fretwell, Elizabeth Greene, Kath MacLean, Andrea Thompson and Russell Thornton for their friendship and support within the wider literary community.

Thanks to Dorothy Cummings and Mark McLean for inviting me to stay with them at Newhailes. The sequence of poems set in Scotland would never have come into existence otherwise!

Much gratitude to James Latrobe for the evocative cover image.

Thank you to my parents, Allan and Holly Briesmaster, for always believing in me.

ABOUT THE AUTHOR

Clara Blackwood is a poet, visual artist and tarot reader. Her first poetry collection, *Subway Medusa* (2007), was the inaugural book in Guernica Editions' First Poets Series, which features first books by poets thirty-five and under. Her poetry has appeared in Canadian and International journals. She lives in Toronto.

Praise for Her Work

Each poem is a rite of passage between the pillars of light and shadow where old and new worlds converge. Blackwood distils fresh insights with clarity and conviction; and although the path is often perilous, we are assured "beauty persists," that magic and mystery are at the root of creation.

— Lea Harper

Clara Blackwood's poetry creates images and patterns that embody the texture of reality. She makes structures incarnating the complexity of consciousness and the transfiguring power of memory. Her poems present the juxtaposition of the ancient and the modern, the appearance of the sacred in the mundane, the relation of nature to mind.

— Len Gasparini

Printed in November 2013
by Gauvin Press,
Gatineau, Québec